LYRICALLY JUSTIFIED

(Volume Two)

By Urban Word Collective

Building futures, Bridging divides

LOTTERY FUNDED

Supported using public funding by

ARTS COUNCIL ENGLAND

LYRICALLY JUSTIFIED
(Volume Two)

By Urban Word Collective
Compiled by Shaun Clarke

© 2017 Urban Word Collective

ISBN: 9781912092574
First published in 2017 by Arkbound Ltd (Publishers)
Cover image by Shamile Haline and Emily Godwin

Arkbound is a social enterprise that aims to promote social inclusion, community development and artistic talent. It sponsors publications by disadvantaged authors and covers issues that engage wider social concerns. Arkbound fully embraces sustainability and environmental protection. It endeavours to use material that is renewable, recyclable or sourced from sustainable forest.

Arkbound
Backfields House
Upper York Street
Bristol BS2 8QJ
England

www.arkbound.com

LYRICALLY JUSTIFIED

(Volume Two)

Contributors

1. SAJU AHMED – Stone Home
2. DAN AUDIO – Be the Change
3. NATHANIEL BENSON - Crimson sky
4. KELLY BOYLE – Love All That You are
5. MESHACH R BRENCHER – Climate Change
6. ROGER GRIFFITH – In search of a King, Identity, and My Kings as Heroes
7. TOM BURGESS – Evolution as Elevation and The Universe is as BIG as My Heart
8. JOHNNY ALBROW - Celf
9. HENNA CANPOETRY – Days
10. ANNDELORIS M. CHACON – Giver and Receiver and Love… Listen… Share!
11. MILES CHAMBERS – I Wanna Be Treated Normal and Are you feeling hot, hot, hot?
12. LUCY CLARK - When a Packet of Space Raiders was 10p
13. MAMA D – Fearlessness
14. STEVE DEEGAN – Safe as Houses
15. JOEL DOUGLAS – Lyrics and Shade
16. SUKINA DOUGLAS – Black Girl Twirl
17. SHAREEFA ENERGY – Inner Peace
18. //KABBO FERDINAND – An Ode to the Mask I Wore
19. JASMINE KETIBUAH FOLEY - Tell us your Stories

Contents

Acknowledgments

Humungous thanks to everyone who helped to make this happen:-

To the Publisher Arkbound, Crowdfunder supporters of our 2017 campaign, which raised over a third of our target: Barry Clarke, Becs Griffiths, Emmanuelle Guerinet, Gyn Smith, Frances Macfarlane, David Milward, Glen Darby, Rohan Cook, Chris Bishop, Renate Schipper, Claudette Clarke, Kev Bunn, Alison Gordon, Jane Cooney, Goosh, Barbi Lukas, Pete Concheeney, Nigel Boney, Michael Thaxter, Kath Hockey, Chris Bishop, Renate, Mike Steel, Jane Cooney, Craig Daveridge, Rohan Cook, Lee Gorman, Nick Halahan, and Mo Secka.

To those who contributed funding and other key work: Arkbound Publishers, Arts Council England, MO Shop, David Ward, Nigel Boney, Chris Bishop – not to forget our families for tolerating our perseverance!

Also thanks to Lauren Living Harrison for your efforts and encouragement, Diverse Arts Network and Ujima Radio for the exposure, and PoetintheCity for the extra support.

We are also grateful to Peter Kalu, Shirley May, Lawrence Hoo and Miles Chambers, FAWOHODIE, Tom Burgess and other friends and partners, including;

REAL YAP PROJECT (Hull)
Full Flava Connection Show (Hull)
DMAC UK
Streets to the Boardroom (Bristol)
Poet in the City (London)
Harbourside Festival Poetry Tent (Bristol)
Commonword Cultureword (Manchester)
Leeds Young Authors
Young Identity (Manchester)
Freedom of Mind (Bristol)
Hive South Yorkshire
BBC Bristol & Humberside
RISE Women (Bristol)
Diverse Artists Network (Bristol)
Co-Resist & Co-exist (Bristol)
The Hydro Bookshop
Spike Island (Bristol)

Finally – to all those who will buy this book and support the cause. We hope that these poems will inspire change and encourage creativity.

Preface

"Poets are the unacknowledged legislators of the world…"
Percy Shelly (A Defence of Poetry, 1821)

"Being part of Lyrically Justified has inspired me, helping my self-expression, poetically and lyrically."
KayB (Lyrically Justified Volume 1)

Converging again with eclectic poetry and prose for the masses, this book involves non-traditional writers. It's about raw and optimistic rhyme and reason, inspired by our times. Depending on the page it may be glad or sad, humorous or deep. It is often rhythmical, but always powerful.

This Urban Poetry anthology provides a fresh platform to promote brilliant, reflective writers who are committed to detangling a tumultuous world. It addresses political and socio-economic problems facing humanity, challenging injustice while questioning human behavior and provoking action.

Lyrically Justified connects UK-based poets from diverse cultural and racial backgrounds, who are empowered to collaborate further and to promote the book independently.

Contributors to Volume One (2016) have commented:

"Superb new platform. Inclusive for unconventional writers of our time."
Steve Duncan

"Lyrically Justified supports young poets by providing an opportunity to publish their work alongside more established poets."
Nadinne Dyen

"Engaging in themes usually excluded from typical poetry."
Marvin Rees, Mayor of Bristol 2017

Volume Two adds to the growing community of artists making sense of the world and building a network, remaining an inspiring platform for positive change.

Let Me Write…

By Ricky Venel Stone

Let me write a soul poem, a travelling poem,
A poem going places, a poem about people,
About good, about evil,
A poem simple at its core,
About my life and about yours.

Let me write a love poem about the pains of love and loss,
About the cost of living to love and loving to live,
About giving not to receive,
But when receiving,
Knowing when to give.

Let me write a cliché poem, a head wrap, eloquent street rap poem,
A beat box, revolutionary head nod poem,
A prose poem,
An old poem,
A heated, hot, warm, cold poem.

Let me write an English poem, a distinguished poem,
A poem that doesn't mince with words,
An absurd poem,
A kiss the sky and hope to die before I try too hard poem.
Let me write a poem.

Let me write a poem about pigs and their wings,
Of policemen who do messed up things.
How each human must walk their own path,
A poem about the wicked, the bad, and the beautifully sad.

Let me write a poem about freedom,
A free myself so I can be more than self-poem,
A flow so righteous you've got to stand up and unite for this poem.
Let me write a poem.

Let me write a poem for the inside of your heart,
The lines to your favourite song,
The poetic drivel in a greetings card that some keep forever,
While others throw them away the very next day.

Let me write an amazing poem, a praised poem, an ego poem, a vent poem,
A bent poem, a straight poem, a zigzagging repaint rainbows.
I hate this poem - No, I love this poem.
I can't make my mind up poem.
Let me write a nice poem, a good vibes poem,
A back to my tribe organ grind poem,
A beat poem, a drum lick, kick of my feet poem,
A deep poem for the shallow-minded poets and a poem for the poets who don't know they're deep.

Let me write a poem for the unknown poets,
The bedroom poets, the open-mic poets.

The poets who can really write poems.
Let me write a poem.

Dislocation

By Lawrence Hoo aka Hoo Law

Human categorisation is creating the declassification of our indigenous nation.

How did we go from…
One world, One people, One nation
To so much separation, segregation and devastation

Mongoloid, Negroid,
Australoid, Caucasian,
European, American,
African, Asian…

Nigerian, Chinese,
Jamaican, Brazilian,
Muslim, Buddhist,
Hindu, Christian…

Black, White,
Mixed, Albino
Dreadlocks, Curly,
Straight, Afro…

Human categorisation,
Is used to divide the masses, for the few,
For multi-levelled manipulation.

Tiny Mountains

By Rebecca Tantony

For the single parent
eating skinny so her children grow
into something richer than those shopping receipts.
For last years school shirts, small feet
and huge dreams.

We are moving tiny mountains together.

For the widow.
For the silence so loud it speaks
for weeks on end of the emptiness
their room shouts since his death.
For her smile, regardless, that smile
so wide the earth sits in the basin
of her mouth and whispers life.

We are moving tiny mountains together.

For his depression.
Wanting to change dead-ends
for motorways, a man so brave and bright
the sun blushes on arrival,
aware of all that quiet light
that illuminates in the centre of his skin.

We are moving tiny mountains together.

*

For it is from those potholes we stand tall
and shout caution to no-one.
These fun, sun-hung mornings
knowing we can see further from up here.
That the darkness was never anything to fear,
just full up of places to play hide-and-seek.

We are worth more than we think.

Hold everything close and climb steep.
Remember ourselves as golden,
as the promises we swore to keep
counting triumph on one hand
and the heartbeats in our chests,
until tiny mountains become cathedrals,
our bodies places to pray hard.

*

For Palestine, the men fighting a weary battle,
the children with skin as beautiful as tree bark.
For Gaza, the women with hearts exploding
as unpredictably as landmines,
for the unrequited romance,
his mouth an unsent love letter.

For the presidents with eyes

empty as motels, for all the girls
who think hip-hop's for boys,
and the boys who think they are too weak
to ever speak in sentiment.
For the teenagers with barbwire
barriers to their voices,
voices that will never, ever fade.

For the overworked and the underpaid,
for getting up regardless of the tired,
for feeding mouths,
bloodshot eyes and yawning.

I wrote this for us all.
And the tiny mountains we climb daily,
so to see how far we have come
and how much more
there is left to discover.

Donna Quixote

By Waltraud Popischil

No, I'm not mad:
> But I am Donna Quixote!
>> A proud woman chasing after real,
>> important dreams.

No, I'm not escaping:
> I am Donna Quixote!
>> Have more brains than all the top
>> psychiatrists' squeezed into one.

No, I'm not ignored by you for being a crazy, annoying
woman:
> I am Donna Quixote!
>> I know you are just kept imprisoned by
>> demons.
But don't worry you beautiful, enchanted, divine image of
an angel:
>> I'll fight all windmills till they turn against
the lying wind...
> I will skin all the wolves of their fake fleeces,
>> So you see the real faces of who told you to avoid
me...

I'll fly through the sky on wings made by my imagination...
> Every shed will be a castle,
>> Every slave will be freed,

Every folly will be eternal truth...

My invincible weapon is eternal love,
   My invincible shield is eternal trust in you...

I won't be taken for a ride by demons plaguing me with
false illusions that:
- I lost you forever - You don't like me - That I am just a
crazy woman - laughed at by all...
No, never, this universe and you deserve better!
              Don't worry, don't cry, and don't shy away...

Because I am Donna Quixote!
            Will rescue you!
   Will rescue our whole world...
            I dream the impossible dream,
As others give in to their nightmares....
      I reach for the impossible star,
            As others take broken splitters of distorting
mirrors for stars...

I am not mad,
         Just the only one who sees that it's madness which
         others take for reality...
                          And once I have rescued you
from the demons that hold you,
   I will also rescue you from the demons *you* hold on to...

You will be there,
         At last, in front of me,

Shaking with laughter….
About a stupid woman like me…

Shaking off all your self-selected demons that way,
And I will be so happy to see you at last…
Just laughing and being amused!

No need to shake my hand,
Or even say 'hello'…
I never asked for more, than to be able to
stop worrying about you,
And see you in a good mood.

I Wanna Be Treated Normal

By Miles Chambers

I wanna be treated normal, whatever normal means.
Have an ordinary life and an ok time.
When friends say "How's work, the family, and the house?"
I wanna say "Just fine."
I don't wanna keep beating you up about our history
I want everything to be safe and cool man I loved to see
genuine unity.
Many injustices done in the present and past, But all this
anger and resentment cannot last

I'm tired of you thinking I've got an attitude,
Chip on my shoulder, like I'm rude
I like to chill out with you,
Have a laugh,
Eat all kinds of funny grub,
I like to go clubbing, bust some moves,
Have a drink in a pub.
I said I just wanna be normal, whatever normal means!
I don't wanna keep seeing black and white
I wanna relax...
Not worry about getting stopped by Police late at night
I don't wanna walk past an elderly lady and watch her hold
tight to her purse
I don't wanna walk into a job interview and
have them look at me as if I've been cursed

I don't wanna read their thoughts when they think he's just like the ones on TV
Is he gonna sell me a ten bag, or get really violent with me
I wanna love a Woman; maybe we'd have sex,
Maybe we'd be celibate like monks in a monastery,
Maybe we'd go at it like rabbits,
Or maybe just a kiss once a day at half past three
Maybe she be black or maybe white
Maybe she'd slack or pray every night

I don't wanna be taken to her house, meet her Dad and hear him shout
"I don't want that sort in here, now get that black bastard out."
I'll have my kids go to some posh school in Clifton, take 12 GCSEs
I want them to pass with flying colours and have their pick of the best universities
Not get in 'cause they're Black, White, Blue or Pink, to get through
But be given an entry 'cause of what they can do
I wanna grow old next to an old English log fire,
Pipe & slippers from Marks & Spencers,
A fluffy cat…

I like to listen to Beethoven and Bob Marley, RnB, Gospel Music,
Have the Lion of Judah on my living room mat.
I don't wanna debate on Proportional Representation,
Positive Action and all that old hat

Define my Identity by ticking some box, like some misguided prat
I'm tired of being a number a statistic of belonging to this and that ethnic group

I wanna be recognised as normal, play football on Sundays
Eat boiled down chicken and oxtail soup!
I like vending machines,
Rubicon Mango Juice and Jamaican fruit Punch!
Love Jerk chicken sandwiches, and Curry Goat flavour Pot Noodle for my lunch.
I like to know that all my Bredren, Spa's, my Idrin, my Bonafide,
My mates, friends – if they wished, could get a degree,
And get high-powered jobs in the financial centre of London City
Or become decision making executives on network TV.

Am I being realistic, or is it not that kind of place?
Do we have to make a big deal of appearances and our race?
Is my colour the first thing you will always see?
Tell me – what is it that you notice when you first look at me?

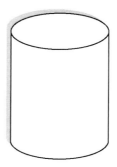

Work Through Me

By Charmaine Lawrence

I ask the source to work through me
For I am a beautiful reflection
A particle of the divine
A speck of greatness within the abundant universe,
For I am the ultimate expression
I am his creation in motion
The vessel that brings forth thoughts from other realms

I ask the source to work through me
For I have a responsibility to humanity
To spread joy, love and wisdom
To listen, learn and teach
To discover the magic
And do the unthinkable,
Challenge me beyond known limits
Guide me through the storms
To shine a light on the bridge of faith,
Connecting past and future,
Over my river of fears

I ask the source to work through me
And be confident and bold,
Compassionate and understanding
To plant seeds deep that will blossom a fruitful legacy
That will allow me to live forever

I ask the source to work through me.......
Naturally,
I wouldn't have it any other way.

Plucked

By Cleo Lake, aka Scota Ronin

A poem inspired by Lubaina Himid's 'Name the Money'
artwork within the navigation charts exhibition.

Plucked
Plucked.
Plucked by a heavy hand and placed here then, here now
Plucked out of the plenty of our motherland's bounty
Of roaming meadows,
Flowers, trees, valleys and vines
Plucked by an empty necessity to create all that was
unnecessary
But for the chosen few base figures,
History rewritten Charts now as underhanded sign off at the
highest level
May I
Lean my head to the side with sad lowered eyes
May I step back in a most courteous curtsey?
May I...
NO!
Adieu
Adieu
I wave my hanky with sad lowered eyes
But as I wave I believe
I believe into the particles of air moving at MY command
Rousing the spirit in space

The concrete of my condition smashes against my skeletal pride

When I stand as I do as a cut out copy of myself

Get the violins out for yourselves

Bow out once and for all roll over and in the rich bounty of the meadows,

Flowers, trees, valleys

The roaming vines

And. Hang. There.

This Disconnect

By Alexia Lindsay aka Humble Be

Ha! A laugh can be a joyous thing
Your assumption leaves room for very little.
A laugh can be a joyous thing
Your assumptions leave little room for something over
nothing
Our interactions prove more distractions
Ah! This disconnect!

All I had said is
You're focused on the poetry
That's when you retort for me to find my own
As said before I wish to lift you up
out of the dirt
How much we could have grown will remain unknown
Alas! This disconnect!

I plead with you
Do not lessen my spirits
It hurts my soul as you refuse to hear this
As you play with verses resounding
So close to connection
My heart is pounding
Imperfect disconnection.

Black Womanhood

By Dareece James

Where to start?
Surveying my bookshelves I see that black women
have said and say so much
in so many spheres
About Black Womanhood and so much more

I think about discussions
in classrooms, kitchens, living rooms, online
at my great-grandmothers bedside
Specific stories that feed into shared experiences and
sacrifice

I have to remind myself
That Black womanhood to me is what I make of it
Though I'm often overwhelmed
by self-appointed gatekeepers of its representation
Is it possible to see value in both bell hooks and Beyoncé?
See agency in the writings of academics, activists and in the
business savvy of reality TV stars and rappers?

Black womanhood
Something so diverse, powerful and potent
I sometimes feel unworthy
Cautious to claim something so precious

Black womanhood means fighting for everybody
Sometimes at the expense of ourselves
Too frequently denied the foreground
Humanity has so far to go

But what gains would have been made
without the time, money, patience and prayers of Black
women?

Black womanhood
is fragile
Sometimes it seems like
success is not always success for black women
but a threat to others

Presumed heterosexual
Some would tell us that we
bear the responsibility for holding black men's attraction
We must not intimidate them with our resolve and financial
responsibility
Some have said that the independence of black women
threatens rather than fortifies the black family
If black women are single mothers, some would tell us
one mis-step could turn our sons to so-called subversive
sexualities and lifestyles

Black womanhood to me

Means claiming vulnerability
in spite of those who would claim it so readily
Yet deny it to us

It means
Meandering with Audre Lorde through her biomythography
Following the Red Dust Road with Jackie Kay
Meeting Nina Simone's Four Women
Figuring out why the caged bird sings

It means seeing
That despite efforts at reductionism

Despite the media and other institutions trying confine us
by stereotypes
Black women continue to complicate the narrative
Whether in the White House or in hip hop videos

It means
Appreciating us in our entirety
Our voices, words, art and aesthetics
Not in particular instances or singularly
Not only when said or worn by someone else
Or said by certain people at certain times

Black womanhood
More than me and my poem
More than I could hope to encapsulate
So consider this a paragraph
In the ever-continuous essay
That is
Black womanhood

Requiem for a Dream

By Hannah M. Teasdale

I have a problem with identity -
in finding a place, a community
where I can slip seamlessly between
textured layers of cultural complexity.
Because my history, my ancestry, gives me
only sharp contrasting fragments
of relationships disintegrated by hatred:
An atheist, champagne-socialist mother
and a misogynist, emotionally absent father
who took bribes in the shadows
of every kind of dealer from the filthy
streets of the Jewelry Quarter.

Sunday was special – in its own dysfunctional way:
Trussed up to impress – skirt and blouse itching
the entire drive down to granny's – wrestling with
conscience
in my father's shimmering-gold Ford Cortina.
11am pick up, sharp, army trained,
he never gained the art of negotiation
and communication came
in the slamming of a horn.
Eight hours of silence screaming
through my head; one-way conversation
both there and back
until dropped at the corner

twenty steps to mum
in a tornado of tears.

But tell me, whose childhood didn't play out
in some version of this?

I say I'm from Birmingham -
Yet no-one hears it.
Any trace of accent slapped out
on a scholarship place
between the tin shelters of private school lockers.
But I found solace at the back of the office
and city centre skate parks -
hanging with lads who had me
for every type of blow.
Smoking, snorting, drinking, puking up our guts
For nothing but to form our own community -
Our own gang of moon-clipped debauchery.

Rave culture of the nineties – identity
found inside a stinking pair
of Fila trainers. No-one asked
Where you came from,
what street you lived in -
no questions asked, no answers given
our mouths too dry for the rigour of conversation.
The sharing of water bottles,
our Holy communion -
God as our DJ, Heaven our dance-floor,
Faithless, our anthem

And at 6 in the morning, we burned incense and prayed
that our minds weren't bending too out of shape.

Millennium exploded and we spun our different ways -
shooting our arrows before giving thought
to our aims. Scattered in pieces across numerous cities:
Manchester, Liverpool, London, Leeds -
Cities steeped in history, cultural identities
we failed to embrace. Poverty, riots, discrimination
marginalization, religious divisions,
boxing clubs, knife crime, sky-scraping flats
and rows of burnt-out shops.
Whilst Tony Blair's meritocracy
bled out to the suburbs.
Regeneration masking ingrained social class
Friends reunited blighted
by golf club dinners and Wimbledon meet-ups.
So, resigned to expectation,
I fled - shot to the 'softer' south-west
in search of a cotton wool future
to settle down and have kids.

And is any Bristol different? For better or worse...
because behind the brightly-coloured brick-stacks
of Totterdown, and the uniformity of Bradley Stoke,
from Bedminster High Street to the Clifton Downs,
Youth groups in Knowle to the edges of St Pauls,
you can find without looking, the same lost souls
still seeking acceptance from the streets where they walk.

Does every place look the same
when you're disengaged? When the youth of today
play more Minecraft than arts and crafts
In times when Assassin's Creed, GTA, and Call of Duty
Are blatantly more significant than their brutal reality?
They chat with snaps, converse in streaks -
A bleak outlook to have when rejected with a swipe.
They will never know what is to 'knock'
for a friend because they're lying in the dark
counting their Facebook 'likes'.

What would you like for your future?
Be a 'better' person:
Be wealthier, greener, healthier, slimmer?
To know your neighbour by name,
And not just by sight?
For your grandmother not to worry
if she remembered
to double-lock her door at night?
To be a better parent, sibling or wife?
To vote for the interests of others
but perhaps not your own?
To not judge intellect by the number of piercings
or the neck hidden by tattoos?
To come to church on a Sunday
to balance out those sins?
To meditate at sunrise to begin the lifelong
process of accepting your own skin?

Because the future will feel bleak

when every path looks the same.
Should we even look at the outside -
at the infrastructure around us,
the industries that trap us
but also saves lives?
Does it matter where we live -
behind which bricks and mortar,
should we compare the road we reside
with the one we think to ought to?

Because we take ourselves wherever we go.
So before we stare out of our windows
seeking someone else to blame,
let us tear ourselves from the inside,
rip open our own minds, see the reflection
looking back in our loved one's eyes.
And come back to them next Sunday,
and again and again
until our own sense of worth becomes
Our Shared Requiem for a Dream.

Power

By Lawrence Hoo aka Hoo Law

Stop giving away your power!
We are not born to be food for others to devour...
We are created from a seed that was given life,
Due to one being coming together with another,
Like bees passing pollen from flower to flower.

And through this natural act of attraction and desire,
We are given life as oxygen feeds our fire,
So don't allow others to extinguish your existence, light or
tire,
Because no matter how low you may feel today,
With just a little self-belief and drive, you can raise your bar
higher.

This Moment

By Rob Mitchell

For Giles & Michelle.

Remember…
That moment we had when we connected?
On touch, we open to clarity…

Your frequency reaching me
Where faults are features, and all thoughts our teacher.
Seeing you, hearing you, feeling you,
Sensing that touch of the Infinite in you!
Remember?

From then, to the now, to the time to come
Let's make *that* 't h e s e,'
More moments, this everlasting.
From then, we will extend
And build momentum.

Let us take many mortal breaths together,
Open to me, as I do, look to me as eye to you,
As we look up to feel the message,
Of Togetherness –
Loneliness – Conquered!

A duet blessed with Gaia's forces,
Drawing down an orchestra to play tunes,

For soothing the soul of this age.
Unashamedly Us
Sealed with Trust.

With you I can conquer the curse of modernity.
You are always my novelty.
You are always new action to jazz up my play.
So – let's stay in this soul-to-soul set,
On course to an era, beyond time and century.

I'm so feeling you, joyfully, holding me gracefully.
Let's pirouette and thrust, through the snakes and the
ladders of the mundane,
Deal with the divots in unkind wickets,
And bad nights, and flights, as they were meant.
As the yin to the yang.

With Strength in the We thing,
Let's win perspective by keeping our senses
On the bigger prize, in the practice of partnership divine.
And together my love, my extended family, my loving
friends. Let's joyfully blend into this moment
Everlasting...

Black Girl Twirl

By Sukina Douglas

The most dangerous words, to have ever been uttered
To women who grace the face of this Earth
Is that your existence is a curse
Your presence drenched with the stench of insignificance
Such fatal words. It's even worse
If the sun has a thing, for the skin that you're in
Black, Brown, Gold and glistening
Becomes a prison that you're living in
Your worth lessens as you increase in melanin
Exoticised and denigrated,
Characteristics exaggerated
Culture appropriated, you are paraded,
Like a savage...
Until your Blackness becomes high fashion
Vogue Magazine, Kim Kardashian, next season
Exploitation of Africans on the runway
Until they find another culture to play with

My culture ain't nothing to play with.
It's even worse, if you're a woman who frequents the
Mosque or Church
Synagogue or nature reserve in search
Of the Sacred,
Backwards and unintelligent is the brush she is painted
with.
In contrast to the construct of 'white, male and atheistic'

A black female who has tasted the Greatness of God
Is seen as the bottom tip of an inverted pyramid
One step lower and she ceases to exist.
But we resist, we resist, we resist
You thought you pushed us down
But we planted our seeds in the ground
And flipped it, came back with Black Girl Magic
Black Orchids, Black Roses, Black Tulips, Black Daisies
I raised me from the pits, a dark dream where you enslaved me
Memories from ancient Mothers and melodies from the unseen
Came to remind me
Not just to seek Divinity but *be* Divinity
Wear the galaxy like a gown to guard your modesty
And dance like the universe in ecstasy

And Twirl, Twirl, Twirl
Twirl for the black girls taught to hate their kinky curls
Twirl for the indigenous women ripped from the Earth
Twirl for the mothers whose children were stolen at birth
Twirl for women who stand on street corners to survive
Twirl for those who sacrificed, to bring forth new life

We are the Black of the universe before the creation of light
We are Black like the Kiswa that covers the Kaaba
Stitched with scriptures of gold
Like the calligraphy sketched on my soul
Our souls more elegant that a thousand butterflies in flight
Newly emerged from the black of their cocoons

We are women in tune with the full moon,
New moon, orange moon, blood moon
Our time will come soon, we just have to remember our
tune.
You just have to remember you.

There is no life here without you
No-one enters this Earthly realm without living in a lagoon
in your womb
This womb, round like sun at high noon
The angels blew and Allah knew
The place to house a new soul is inside you
Prophets and paupers
Baptised in these sacred waters
Between heaven and earth, we are the portal
Eternity embedded in a mortal
We are beautiful and awful
Extraordinary cloaked in a mortal.

The revolution will start, when we activate the heart
We are Rosa Parks and Joan of Arc
We are Empress Menen and Tawakkul Karmen of Yemen
We are Queen Nefertiti, Amy Garvey and a maroon called
Nanny
We are Rabia al Adawiyya, Queen Nzingha, Winnie Mandela
and St Teresa of Avila
We are Betty Shabazz wife X
We are Aminah Umm Muhammed
Khadijah Zawjatun Muhammed
Fatima Bint Muhammed

The feminine face and fragrance of her father
We are the women Sahaba, women of the sahara and the
savannah
Women of the Islands and of the concrete
Women of the townships and of the cities
We are women of our own destinies

The ropes around our tongues, will only become undone
When we cut them!
Then we will Twirl, Twirl, Twirl
Twirl through the battle scars, labour pain and broken
hearts
Twirl to give birth to a new Earth before we are devoured
Twirl until the final hour
Twirl like the moon's cycle
Twirl because we are our last chance for survival

We must twirl, twirl, twirl.

Alone-liness

By Rob Mitchell

Loneliness is what we had to begin with
Lone, Lone, Lone,
Alone, alone,
All-one-li-ness,
All we,
The royal we of course.

Sorry!
Did I say 'we',
Or was that 'me',
Or 'I'?
I is a playful tool.

The ghoul to fool the one,
Into forgetting the loneliness,
So that I and you,
Can play who's who,
On the Earth board.

Where me, and she, and he, and it, collide,
Take sides, creating boundaries –
Us and them diversities,
I plays red *and* I plays blue,
Or black and white - it doesn't matter,

Cos I is you too.
We know of course

That I and I make two
From one indivisible one-ness
True?

Evolution as Elevation

By Tom Burgess

"I'm not after religion! I want mercy"
Said Jesus
No one listened and on it went

So as a child I worried when I forgot to start god with a
CAPITAL
Yet neglected my natural wonder
And was blind to my blessed life
Gratitude did not exude, it was fleeting
I wanted my next fix

In the addled essence of adolescence
Performance poured
So on it went
The drama of a personal universe
Taking license with the script, ad lib
Always half an eye on the prompts
Who waited in the wings like hovering vultures
Ready to devour stray ideas
Screeching lines like that was all there was

As an adult
Other people's voices still echo in my inner cathedral
Though truth be told
I could never say everything
I would always stumble over the punch line

Honestly
I revere justice too much to make myself it's depository

Come to the party, everyone
Respond without judgment, let go
Police others thoughts no longer
No more will you vanquish all that threatens you
Give up on being so correct
Deal in real and make room for mercy.

Free-dem Fighters

By Nattylyn Jeffers

We are de new generation of Free-dem Fighters,
Seeking to combat and eliminate the injustice of modern
society in de 21st Century AD as we know it.
We are awake.
We are alive!
As Dawn breaks and de Sun sets, we bless de Moon and
Mother Nature for revealing her true magnitude of majestic
powers.
We battle with true consciousness in dis weary time of Isms
and Schisms, in a time of a mass blackened fog,
We nah like "Willy Fogg" travelling through the blunders of
a global land with no master plan.

Free-dem Fighters, getting up, standing up, fighting for our
rights.
We nah stand still, till de work is dun!
De Motto: Elimination of destruction...
Elimination of poverty and sustained suffrage - injustices...
We do it our own way, with our know-how.
We protest in peace, love, and intellectual over-standing.

De new generation of Free-dem Fighters,
Using new technologies to seek each other out,
From de back broken miners back home to de back broken
workers of dis modern slavery...

We nuh afraid – we nah show fear as we unite in global unification – we have Arts, we have souls.
Let de Spirit awaken,
I n I need nuh modern Witch Docta!
Liberate our Brethren and Sistren, living in a Zombied state of subconscious pain.
Show empathy for those facing the living nightmare of foolishness,
Caused and inflicted by Babylonia.

We are de new generation of Free-dem Fighters, taking tings into our own hands,
Like child Souljahs we walk weary yet…
We are not blind to see what is being asked of us;
We are prepared to sacrifice ourselves,
Knowing we are doing de rightful ting for ourselves and others.
It's de start of World War Tree…
For we - de new rebel fighters,
Conquering Lions and Lionesses of Judah,

We march with our pickney for de future generation.
Righteous Buffalo Souljahs, marching for Free-dem!
All with a duty in dis "New World Orda",
Visualising de new society created by Skulduggery Pleasant,
We must all play our part in de New Light, de New Hope,
In order to reach mass salvation and Livication!
Let us go fourth in de creation of de New Nile,
When we reach de-land of gold richness and natural spoils,

WE - will be blessed in de knowing that –

WE - are Back Home!

Where deh is no economic inequality and racial division...

In dis true promised-land, de living nuh dead...

There is no #death in #paradise.

And as we lay - resting,

We pass de baton onto de next Free-dem Fighters...

"Dulce et Decorum est"...

Your Calling

By Chloë Rose Laing

Is it 'cause we're born to wake up?
And understand the roads of man,
That breed an evil that's so real,
Or is it 'cause we're born to wake up?

To comprehend the roads of man,
That fund an evil that's so damn real.
Divide and rule,
Some cast a seed then left them gruelling,
Down-pressor, know that the truth,
It is never gonna give up!

Soul's grounded, to a river,
Flowing roots and culture,
So we feel beneath the concrete and the pavement,
For our lines ancestral,
And our rights.
Without your calling where would you be now?

Another shock,
Soul gets locked up,
Another mother's son caught out!
What about conscience?
We're separating from our core within, existing...
Without your calling where would you be now?

So – on daughters, go on,
On and on daughters, go on,
We keep on bearing children.
We keep on bringing forth life,
Looking for the light in his eyes,
Looking for the light above his left shoulder.
You and I...

Is the answer in somebody else?
What I prove to myself?
Cries of our foremothers and fathers?
Living inner unity?
Is the answer consoling our divinity?

The light shines always to brighten another day.

Safe as Houses [LS6]

By Steve Deegan

In the City of Leeds, specifically Woodhouse,
This was where we lived, and this was where we doled out,
A labour of love, to keep our conscience alive,
To keep our eyes peeled, and not get side-tracked
By the corporate illusion, so thinly veiled,
And in squats we mapped out our dreams, so Safe as
Houses.

And sat there in the corner, in your patchwork scarf,
We thought you'd cut it, perform in the dark,
And you had the spark, the idea of your choosing,
But you kept living on the edge to escape the delusion.

In the City of Leeds, specifically Hyde Park,
This is where we dwelled, and this is where we stood out,
To cut the mustard, not stand in the dole queue,
With your pie-eyed gaze, hazed in the dream hue,
Of the night after the morning before...

...Feeling so forever sure that market forces won't corrupt
our work,
That we still won't be jaded, and carry on through the
gloom,
Only to find ourselves sipping from a retro coffee cup,
In the vintage market e-kingdom,

The boho-chic parade,
Where with your blood brother you collide,
To stop your craft from corroding,
And then you know you're Safe as Houses.

Days

By Henna CanPoetry

I have days that ignite my soul
Drag me to infinity
Break me in two,
Then make me whole
Days I want to run away,
Pack a suitcase, leave, depart
Far, far, away in search of a better day.

I have days where my emotions are left in my dreams
And I find myself feeling numb, and ridiculously empty.
Days I...
Sink in a bloodbath of long lost dreams,
As my soul bleeds in my world of fantasy...

Because some days I just can't face reality.

I have days where I feel the warmth of a forsaken embrace
Stroking my heart whispering 'Darling, You're going to be
ok'.
Days that are just nights, and in the darkness I lay with my
demons,
Crying, laughing,
Trying to find my purpose, my reason.

I have days I dance naked in my pain,

Fiercely, seductively,
Singing away my sorrows
In the cold November rain.
Days I love,
No taking, just giving
Embracing a humanity that's no longer living,
Just surviving.

I have days I watch my hopes and goals from the window
pane
Falling, piece by piece,
As every drop melts
Hysterically, on the December snow.
And I contemplate whether
To pick up the pieces or leave them for another day.

I have days I spark the green, blaze my angels as they fall
apart with my demons.
I sit there anticipating as my world falls apart,
So I sink deep within the last moments of my unforgotten
memories.
Days I want to remember,
And days I want to forget.

But today, I just want to
                              ...Rest.

Be the Change

By Dan Audio

Wake up now and see,
Ride the new wave.
Put down all that fear,
Time to be the change

External, shit's eternal,
Man dem just want me to burn up,
Pay that tax, and boil my bloodstream,
Walk that tightrope, take the vaccines,
Road rage, old age, breathe the chem-trails,
Zap my body with elementals.
Feed that fear, increase the war zones,
Make more guns, bulldoze the kids' homes.

World War Three takes place in your mind...
Do you see a brother, or an Isis fighter?
Do you see a victim, or a crisis actor?
Do you ask a question, or just follow after?
Instinct is the deciding factor,
Does yours work, or is it inactive,
Do you stand strong when a billion are wrong?
Sticking to your point cos you know your points are strong

Deceivers rip to pieces,
Now I see them walk amongst us.
You cannot free them, just advise them,

Newspaper readers lost and mindless.
See them making money and more power,
Every time we are divided...

Wake up now and see,
Ride the new wave.
Put down all that fear,
Time to be the change.

Warrior Queen

By Alyx Tamminen

And she woke up
Hair bed-scuffed, skin to sheets, alone
No better company could prepare her,
For the severing of her heritage.
There's a headstone being stolen
She is never heading home
Through the borders she orders torn down
And the vengeance she buries 'til her belly's full
She knows she's running.

Crazed away from the skeleton inside of her
As sure as she knows she's becoming it,
But she'll keep drumming her feet on new streets,
Keep her eyes on horizons, fingers in fists
No beat missed, no wings clipped

She exists -
Through the struggles and at peace bits.
So when her skin's creased,
Memories are rings of felled trees
And death is at her feet
She'll place a hand on his head, raise it,
Meet his gaze...
And break his neck.

Climate Change

By Meshach R Brencher

What's the forecast for today?
Well you won't be sunburned
But you'll definitely feel the political heat rising
Hypocrisy wearing tailored suits
Declaring manifestos on podiums across the nations
Claim to look out for your people
Once you are sucked into venomous green gases
Spewing saliva about trivia
While ice caps are melting
Dissolving into a river of prejudice
Carrying disposed emissions in packages
Propaganda littering a gateway microscope
Polluting this generation's demographic

Information guarded on sabotaged plantations
Homelessness is a typhoon that hurls empty wallets
Into wishing wells
Washed-away memories of dead bodies
Now competing over media coverage
The real place where the sun rises the most
Exposing heated conversations as the talk of the town
A malice vote to exit a union
That offered a stable structure
Distributed by a rigged finger
Triggering the software

Attempting to detonate the system
Prisoners left playing cards
Cutting a deal to incarcerate our freedoms
While extremists give grievance
Deforestation for radicalisation

Everyday people defined by a single ethnicity
Yet our ancestors sailed through many diasporas
They had predecessors just like you do
In the depth of depression we indulge on vices
Standardised cigarettes give ash the breath
Of hallow mist tipping over your finger
Sanctioned airstrikes vacuum this throne clean
For an evil dictator to take his seat
His massive ego is high octane
That wears a radioactive lab jacket
The logic of combustible elements splurting
Only exhale words through the gaps
Missing teeth are unuttered speech remarks
That only serve tooth decay
Sabotaged information could only fill these spaces
Censorship wears a fist shoved down your throat
The innocent are the ones always left to feel guilty for not
understanding
Failed child upbringing is a cradled theft of possession
Disposed shelter creased and folded up
Within a secret annexe
While bleaching the faceless mask
Underneath the silhouette
No ventilation

Filling the room full of toxins
Expect humid air pressure across many parts of today's
weather
But temperatures are expected to cool down
If (only) we ever settle our differences

Lyrics and Shade

By Joel Douglas aka Splitz P

Building myself like an ancient mason
Reaching new heights, I'm levitating
Scriptures revising, I'm educating
Platinum locks man, there is no breaking
Vivid poetry so u can see the image
Older Rasta man say dis yout is wicked
Searching for truth, I'm constantly digging -
Synchronised with the ancient times, and da ryddim

Living in da concrete jungle is hard
Dis place boosts my ego, make me forget God
Had me lost, wondering da streets like dog
Used to live like a faker and fraud
Searching for truth led me to a different energy—
Reminding myself of death like a cemetery –
And that this world is here temporarily
But love outweighs all hate and jealousy

Social media has di yout-dem on lockdown, Heads down -
thumbs down, spaced out, in a cloud
I phone, I cloud, I you, I now, I straight, I round, Everything
is I now

Individuals with no need for sharing
We do it for the likes, no need for caring
We do it for the comments and social pairing
Trends and fashion has di youts-dem glaring
Everybody living and acting da same
Wearing da same clothes, playing da same games
But they're cold inside, minds filled with rain
Cold... Freezing, for the likes everyday

I'm blessed to have good people around me
Who have a higher energy and think intellectually
Conversations about how to change the world -
With concerns of our women and how they condition girls

To be like them - To be drip fed
Social media death has di youts-dem stressed
Society glorifies a fake lifestyle
Mothers are rewarding their daughters for selfies and
pouts?
What's happened to our people - moving feeble?
We used to be together but now our families are weak

Youts growing up with no Dads and Mums
Looking up to the elders with drugs and guns
Take to the streets and let it bang like drums
Idolising material wealth, funds and sums

They don't teach us our history in school
We're conditioned to conform and be a slave and a fool
Black yutes do trap and carry guns and tools?
It's a crazy world that we're living in
A world built on sin - with everybody trying to win
And be accepted by their online friends
Knowledge of self is priceless, no rubies or gems can take
that away from me,
Viral trends and memes,
Man-dem talkin' 'bout Italian clothes, champagne and
cream...
Bruv, what do u mean? 'Bout Italian clothes
When your local black businesses are near enough broke
We don't invest in our communities, that's why we're slow
to help each other.

We would rather make excuse and moan
When back in the day it was cool to be smart and educated
Whilst knowing your history, I'm not exaggerating

Nowadays I don't understand what rappers say?
They're mumbling with no grace, but rewarded with pay

Passion and talent doesn't pay the bills anymore
Single parent mums feeling strained and sore
They're crying out for help, tryin' to talk to the Lord
But not gettin' no answers, so they fall to the floor
Living in the land of the beast and hidden opportunities
They're disguising ill things as jewellery
From our food and TV diet, to our education
Everything seems flawless so we hardly question

But I keep on travelling through this wind and rain
Becoming closer to the most high makes me feel sane
In general this land comes across as so grey
Don't let this place burn you, my lyrics provide the shade.

Apricity

By Russ Litten

Golden hour at 159, the back yard,
the stubbed out embers of the day.
The tribes of KUH are cooling down,
that ball of fire fading,
the shadow of the basketball hoop
makes a halo on the ground,
plastic Nerf guns melted in a multi - coloured pool,
a radio murmurs two gardens down,
The Isley Brothers, that bumblebee guitar,
distant,
another country.

Somewhere along the ten - foot
a football bangs against a garage door;
it's 4pm in the universe
and I no longer care about cholesterol levels or the
government.
The soul detaches and floats upwards, heat rising;
that pigeon again, with a sudden dart to the rooftops,
settles on the chimney,
cock - eyed,
leaning, as the police helicopter above him buzzes through
blue,
an angry metal dragonfly following the vapour trail
back to the mothership, back to the source.

Boy racers tearing up and down the avenue
and the brown and black
and pink flowers erupting,
the red necks in the beer gardens sinking pints of amber,
the last drop of the afternoon,
getting ready for the night.
The festival in the park is packing up its tents;
a giant struggles to his feet and falls back down again,
no more music leaking through the windows or drifting
down the street,
the drum club near the bandstand meets monthly –
all invited, all intact.

I feel the rhythm from my back yard
but I'm too petrified to move,
I'm burnt red raw, beads of water on glass,
a galleon afloat among the icebergs,
I've got a head full of pollen and these bones are melting in
the heat.
I traded all my earthly worries for a doctor's note and a
mouthful of dust;
summer will be gone soon,
and these golden hours will turn to rust.

An Ode to the Mask I Wore

By //Kabbo Ferdinand

If ever there was a time in his/tory for god to arrive.
I beg, I grovel, I cry, surely it must be Now!
I implore you, please!
Tell me her/story, i think to myself,
That of the liberated being; not yet known.
Ye all gods, know ye not?
A thought lives in my heart,
In wonderment i look on at our state,
Wombman; me & U? While,
The market says: 'starve the tool maker,
Let 'em salivate after a taste of consumer's bliss &
Wa LAH!!!(C'est la vie!) Yes! The reality is like,
A whimpering lament of a devolving species,
Who never warns of its extinction,
For competition ensures the weak of its place.
As true as the hopelessness found on youth in Bristol
Is a carbon copy of that found on youth of cape town.
Channelled via cultural malignant tendencies.
Insidiously spread, if one were too dare to imagine that there's,
Hope in the eyes of today's peasants.

Our purpose, deferred toward a reductionist utopian dream;
Alas! a means to an end within measures of hope.
As this civilised nightmare unfolds, not so long ago,

Ships from these shores had our ancestors cast in chains
Chattel, wilfully sold for profit, Briicqk Stowe, you owe!
Thus, may the seeker be of A questioning type- cast light into dark,
For a seed sprouts with the promise of shade,
As dust & water dances to the tune of gravity,
Each to its own groove faithfully, like the phases of the moon.
If she were to appear, i would rally her to the plight of the wretched,
For the privileged seem to enjoy his favour, Now!
Ladies & Gentlemen! Step On Forth for Today!
We dealing in human misery @ only 30 quid a pop!
Yes! Look at fine subhuman here, sweet like sugar cane.
Never worked a day in the field, perfectly schooled for your entertainment!
You will be the talk of the town with this exotic creature attachment, Guaranteed!!!
Do We Have Any Takers! Yes! No! Why? Move back!
No food for you tonight, you costing me, You Come!
Why My! Look at this 1, My fellow good Christians!
Strong arms, great teeth, it's what we call a Silver Back
His life's worth is profit in your pocket, Guaranteed!!!
They've all been whipped into shape, civilised, abolition insured &
Best of all they come with a built in, do as you please system,
Sir, Madam, it's been ordained, Guaranteed!!!
& so we waved back & forth from 1670's until 1805 & beyond.

Civil blood leaving civil hands unclean, Today, Think? Pray!
Love! Libya!
Silenced trauma is searching for memory's healing voice.
What are you doing? Where have you been?
She visits me, in my dreams at night, always uttering,
urging me on, take off the mask! it's time, time to evolve.
As the veil thins', my masks seem to grow, more
Unfit for purpose, at her beck & call, evolution's quasi
philanderer.
She though cautions balance, patience, ambivalence;
For she embraces benevolence & malevolence without
favour.
Finally, I see, I feel, I hear, now! I sense, I yearn, I know!
Our Earth, she has answers; ever tolerant of our baneful
ways.
Unhinged, the mask slips off, smiling, he stare's back at me
& says: "Now before I hit the floor & break, repeat after me,
//Kabbo the one who dreams;

I Am Universal Harmony!
I Am Universal Balance!
I Am Universal Life!
I Am Universal Love!
I Am That I Am!!!
Evolutionary words, drops, shatters, I swoop to scoop it up,
You've served me well, manna for the uncultured self.
Now every time life asks me I utter this phrase,
Trusting that life is exactly how it is for in the end, you &
me, we'll be fine!

Yes, in deeds, our time is ripe, our generation's chance to blossom &

Honour our potential, honour our women, our children, honour our men,

Honour ourselves, honour our ancestors by making time,

Time to mourn, forgive, heal, evolve, now & only then

Can we restore our species & in doing so, adjust our living equilibrium,

On Earth & in all of the heavens, for in this desire I wrote this ode,

Evoking a stream of emotion that burns through doubt,

Knowing acknowledgement's needed for our individual & cohesive collective healing,

Dare I say, a clean break from these soulless merchant laws & policies is yearned for,

So much so, therefore we know that Reparations is a Must!!!

U & me, wombeings, Yes! We am enough, as true as Love,

(Breathing Deeply) As true as, 1 love!!!

Giver and Receiver

By Anndeloris M. Chacon

To help someone who does not understand they need help,
Is a struggle for the giver.

Methods of getting there will differ...

The receiver sometimes asks for help, but is unsure of what
help is needed.

Both parties struggle...

They find themselves in the dilemma,
Of not accomplishing anything that is mutually beneficial.

The receiver must be clear for the giver to be able to help
them reach their goal.

The goal is where they both should have as common
ground.

But, there are times their methods of getting there will
differ.

So, the giver may have to withdraw and wait.

Love... Listen... Share!

By Anndeloris M. Chacon

Stop and look, and listen!

Love! Listen! Share!
Three beautiful words for life which are interchangeable in
their order.

We can love first which lead to listen then share,
We can listen then love and share?

Some may share and in the process,
Listen and love.

Whichever way we mingle and move these three words,
They will always be present in our lives.

Endless, are the possibilities these words can open for us,
If we open to them.

Love! Listen! Share!

When a Packet of Space Raiders Was 10p

By Lucy Clark

The world was such a better place to be,
When Space Raiders were still 10p.
Or with 50p walk into your corner shop
And leave with change, Kaylie AND a Panda Pop.

Climbing trees, mucky nails and knees
Pre-braces wonky teeth,
Curing any nettle stings
With a single green dock leaf.

A packet of chocolate cigarettes to inhale,
Buying your Dad a green Sports Mail.
Fizzy Astro Belts and Liquorice Whips
Finding Tazos in your Walkers crisps.

Micro Scooters and Raleigh Choppers,
New Nike Air Max teamed with Adidas poppers.
Watching Round the Twist, Saved by The Bell,
Byker Grove, Kenan and Kel

Playing a grey Game Boy that was 2 inch thick,
Or with a constantly shitting Tamagotchi chick.
You'd get 10 Cadburys Freddos for a quid before
Now the same amount will buy you 4.

Bright blue eyeshadows.
Black tattoo chokers made of elastic,
We had massive 50p's back then,
Not fivers made of plastic.

Your first ever alcopop
Bacardi Breezer, Hooch or Reef
A packet of Space Raiders for just 10p
Pickled Onion, obviously, not Beef.

The world was such a better place to be
When Space Raiders were still 10p

Crimson Sky

By Nathaniel Benson

The city is empty.
Dry heat rises from the concrete like dead men.
And there he stood,
Slowly crisping to ash,
Flaking to the ground,
Scorched by the scarlet skies.
And as his remnants scatter across the blazing sin,
A figure relieves him from the left.
"I can feel you burning."

Two lights illuminate the horizon
Slowly moving from our sight,
Walking through corpses wearing carrion crow cloaks
Clasped around their hearts.
Standing entwined like two twisting willows
Weeping for each other

...Naked. Pried open by eyes tinged with the pain and
prejudice
Tears run from the dessert.
Disowned by their motherland,
Lost children
Branded,
Buried,
Burned into them,
A love they cannot kill,
In the fires of a crimson sky.

The Soil

By EmFyahSis MC

See,

I'm growing up; I am a child; here on this Earth/my birth to
now

Makes me just fourteen/

But there have been/ so many things that I have seen

Not all of them I have written down/

But they always stay with me

In my heart/

Of which soil is, of course, the Queen.

Nile Overflow, Ganges overspill

Creating as we go, fertilising as we will

Listen,

The soil was created for different things/

Not just for the benefit of human beings/

Some of us feel as though the Earth is only for us

But others? They don't even make a fuss/

We hardly recognise/what is right in front of
our eyes/

We talk of her as if she's something to
despise/ugh, but that's all lies (that's. all. lies)

Nile Overflow, Ganges overspill

Creating as we go, fertilising as we will

Deep, dark mother soil

Always open, always silent, always still

Nile overflow, Ganges overspill

Creating as you go, fertilising as you will/
Trodden upon/pierced by forks/cut by spades
Prodded, poked and pierced/burnt by harsh
sun rays/
Massaged by the tiniest of hands and feet
and/
Ingested and worked through by the
smallest guts/
Transformed by fungi in many ways/
Sand to silt/ silt to clay/always in flux.
Soil in my hands/dirt at my knees
You have embraced life and held still bodies/
Dirt is a lie/Soil is the Truth
The greatest story ever you tell at the root/
Nile Overflow, Ganges overspill
Creating as we go, fertilising as we will
Nile Overflow, Ganges overspill
Creating as we go, fertilising as we will
Nile Overflow, Ganges overspill
Creating as we go, fertilising as we will
The greatest story ever you tell at the root/the
greatest story ever you tell at the root, at the
root, at the root/the greatest story ever, you tell at the root.

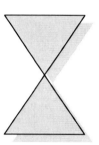

FEARLESSNESS

By Mama D

Fearlessness, where does it come from?
If we don't fear, then surely we won't run?
For isn't running from the core of self -
Celebrate the marathon, like it's for your health.
Old Greek ideas, philosophies, push out all the others -
Fatherland ideas respected, but what about the southern
mothers?

Time to take a stock and bring in all the pluriverse
Acting from your silo, won't that make things worse?
Intergeneration struggles, are they orchestrated?
We are all ancestors and all youth with wisdoms that aren't
rated -
Nor venerated, sometimes even hated.

What values resonate in your soul?
What integrity do you hold?
Where do we go with trust?
So many questions, my head's goin' bust
With IRON-age masculinities
Woh! My blood will rust...!

GMO, to and fro, glyphosate, all down the row
Cancer causing, really emotional
Our backsides/Right inside/The herbicide -
just roller coast-er-nal

When is it going to stop?
Are they waiting for us all to drop?
Like bees and butterflies, and scientific lies
That most of us won't politicize?
We still ain't woke, not opened up our eyes!

Heavy breathing, still believing/People dying, many grieving...

Even when I've done with this rhyme
My thoughts in your head going overtime -
Zero hours contracts, the labours in decline -
The only work for you is bringing out what's in your mind.

Even when this poem's quit you'll be humming with the verse.
To deprogramme you'd best recall, and nurse, each idea slowly in reverse,
Full brain-cell-healing/Not a curse.

My words are feeding you/Not bleeding you/Bring deed in you.

It's a mothering, a nourishing/a mothering/a nourishing.

Can U Feel Me, Not?

By Razor

They got money to upgrade technology
But don't have money for the homeless peeps!
I see someone sleeping on the doorsteps, or the streets,
People going through the bins, doing sins 'cos they need to
eat,
Cold beans through the tins,
I feel guilty,
I don't know why,
'Cos Society is gunna die,
Fry cuz,
What's it all about?

The government won't help the block,
Always see shots,
It don't stop,
People still dying in the ghetto,
Family being sunk at the graveyard,
Rest in peace to all dying souls,
The world needs a saviour,
The ill behavior –
What's it all coming to?

Drug deals,
Thug kills,

Overdose pills, Masons!
It's like we're trapped in hell
People pray in their cells
'Cos that's the only place to cope
The only way is we live on hope
Hoping some God can save us,

It's a dark night and I'm trying to survive
How can we get through this painful life?
Can you hear me? Can u feel me? 'Cos he can't care less.

It's getting to that season where the homeless ain't
breathin'
'Cos they be sleeping in dem freezing cold roadz,
Is there a reason for all of dis?
How did it come to dis?
All the world needs is peace, even for the G's,
'Cos it's getting so Krazy. Living on these streets,
I look to my left, I see a fight,
I look to my right, a dealer in sight
Madness everywhere, even with the feds,
I'm going mad physically, like my head,
I'm getting sick of living, I'd rather be dead,
Look in people's eyes and you will see red,
The world's full of badness,
And madness, with sadness.

It's a dark night for trying to survive
How can we get through this painful life?
Can you hear me? Can u feel me? 'Cos he can't care less.

Bi-Polar

By Lauren Living Harrison

I'm on the way home
I couldn't do it!
"But YOU did it!" she says
Not properly, I reply to the voices in my head
"You could not have made it at all..." She goes on.
Have to look at it like that instead.
All this self-harm is regrettable
If you are not careful,
We will both soon be dead
Now there's nothing worse than that
You're doing your best –
Have to look at it like that, my friend.
Your mind is as delicate as the next –
From the baby, fresh
Out the birth canal saying their first "Hello" to this world,
To the eighty-seven-year-old vet
We must protect it,
Treat it with care.

Abstain from all that media junk
Organic thoughts need a fertile flower bed to
BLOOM into the beauty they are supposed to be,
Without influence from online streams
They follow suit.
You are...
Your thoughts, and

Your thoughts
Are You,
So be careful where you lead them to,
Up the hill and down again.
I believe bi-polar is the term they use?
But just between me and you
I think *THEY'VE got it Wrong!*
Emotions fLuCtUaTe
Like the tide comes in,
And night turns to day,
The cycle of a healthy mind,
A Cycle that they'd like to break.

See you've got it girl! I hear her say
As WE sit alone and CONTEMPLATE.

Emerald City

By Lauren Living Harrison

Just when you think it's all over...
The prickly brown 'Welcome' mat between your toes
STANDING at the doors of Your Utopia.
Your stiff, *deserving* finger rings the bell
Your toes still sinking deeper, further.
Damn! No answer.
You give it a –
Soles trying to determine whether to relax now you've reached,
Or reac*t* to the fact that the texture of this 'welcome' mat
The foundation   you, on which -
                    Beneath
you stand, is part of the reason for your f- rustration now
Your knees are bruised and
Seepin*g*.
But instead of finding the comfort you sought
This Utopia appears to be deceiving.
You start to ponder
Was the road you endured to get here really worth it?
Reality kicking in,
You start to wonder
Is this really a 'Welcome' mat I stand on?...
Or a trap?!
A mirage on your path, as its placement seems strategic
A trap?!
To misguide you in your pursuit of happiness,

Of inner peace
A trap?!
To stop you becoming the best YOU that you can be,
To keep you
                 underneath
A trap?!
To prevent you from getting what you deserve
Getting to that place where You -
                 could be...
                 Forget/Diss/ That!

After all the hard graft you've put in
                 that place where you
                 Should be.

The Universe Is As Big As My Heart

By Tom Burgess

A sense of the broken places presses upon me
Compresses my mind
As my sickly fortune balloons into oblivion
Guilt mixes with bile
I am full of the urgency to love
Oppressed by friends and strangers, all scattered
Slashed at by life's sharp edge
The block stop wedge
A bleak point, without purpose
Pain's hammer, relentless
The inevitable terminus,
Relief?

And me with a sense of hope
A bubble not yet burst
Borrowed eyes still seeing
Recognising life in the presence of its shadow

Oh thick black shape!
I pray that something good billows in your depths
I try to imagine some end to life that is bigger than its parts
Fingers press for blood
The wish a rusty-eyed red scream
It is one
Precious in pain, illusively here
It is not me, why is that so?

I am here, something not
I do not know how to interpret the vague impulses of this
formless monster
So I drift in an absurd world

Love seems my only cause of action
Off runs fear, melancholy drains
Guilt remains
What of those who cannot get hold of anything to navigate
by?
Who have dismantled every story yet cannot tell another
Or the simply tired,
Named or not, those that suffer terribly
Do so quietly

I cannot think for them
Lying sleepless, still breathing
As foolish as when I first entered this world
The thought lingers like a bird with no nest
I was born
The terrifying thrill of it rises in my chest
BORN!

The Ballad of Refuge

By David Punter

I come in fear.
The wheels, the stuttering engine,
By road or wave; the endless killing payments.
Bit by bit, my mind returns to rubble.

You come in fear.
The hunched back, failed bravado,
They make me squirm. You have no place here, brother;
Get back, for you remind me of my weakness.

I starve, I thirst.
I'm out there in my millions,
Teeming, weeping. Just allow me, brother,
One foot on land. I'll work hard for my pittance.

You starve, you thirst.
What of me, of my neighbours,
Struggling in an austere land? The steel plant's silent,
My skills no longer fit, my hands are idle.

My hopes are gone.
My suffering gods won't travel,
My women cannot see, their eyes are blinded
By the long dust, the silent days of torture.

My hopes are gone.

You come and you displace me,
The silent mills and fields, they scorn and mock me,
The Union Jack's a shroud; all's ripe for burning.

I call to you.
Across the long dark waters,
Carrying a load of trinkets not worth selling,
Umbrellas, handbags, at the gang-master's calling.

You call to me.
I stop my ears with plaster,
My sons and daughters can't afford their schooling,
My hospitals are full, the asylum's broken.

My last cry sinks.
Protect me from this hardness,
This cold that shrinks my soul. Pity me, brother,
Or think on me adrift on the long night's calling.

My last cry sinks.
Protect me from this falling.
The bailiffs come, the sheets won't disentangle.
My homeland's gone. God help us all this winter.

Tell Us Your Stories

By Jasmine Ketibuah-Foley

Seeing words collate on a page,
Remembering...

The foretold stories
Of my ancient forefathers and mothers,
Reminds me of how we all communicate freely in this
tongue of history,
So easily misshapen and mistaken in tones and dialects and
new news.
New feelings on one sound vibrating on tongues old and
true.
Communicating with each other,
In a peace unknown to the tangible world,

A whisper,
Cry loud and soft on top of the ears of us
all human.

I can see your words in the air written in your breath,
And falling on my open hands clear,
And chuckling grasping the fire in my belly.
Here as we sit watching the telly,
I note the lines next to your eyes.
A sign the crows still speak of
age,
And stories still to be heard.

Their callous feet creeping into
your grin.

In life we will win,
We will be rich with your wisdom.
Tell us of your kin-dom
Struggles lost and won in one breath of fresh air love.

We don't talk enough
We don't sing or dance enough,
To the silence of life outside bright and green techni-colour
scream,
Technological dreams….We have many…
But I want to hear what you used to do.
To escape back to a freedom of times before I was born…

Before,
When I would have called instead of whatsapp'd you.

Patterns of Behaviour

By Solomon O.B

I'm not being funny but I'm sick and tired of being accused
of accusing someone of being racist
You calling me coloured instead of black is far more
outdated than some of my iPhone apps sand they really
could do with some upgrading
But I'm not calling you racist see,
My foster parents even say it
Nan and Grandad, they're white, I'm black, which makes it
slightly more complicated but not really is pretty basic see,
they're from a generation were racial slur sometimes are
just part of the conversation so I can't really blame them,
But you, you're 4th generation Y so why do you say it?
Especially since you've had the benefit of education
Not necessarily university, just more diversity in this life we
lead and despite these facts your language is more akin to
nursery you follow me?
I get it, people can say some racist shit without necessarily
being inherently racist
My foster parents certainly weren't, they would have taken
on me, my older brother younger sister
All biological on that basis
The whole family embraced us into their hearts the same
way veins take in blood
They were far more concerned with the colour of our
character than the shade of our faces but...

I guess it's far less about the words you say and more about the intent with which you say them

So no! this does not mean you can call me my nigga as a "term of endearment"

Shit I wish I didn't bring this up

This is some of the most over debated stuff

Yes some of us call each other "it"

No I'm not completely defending it

But you have to understand the re-appropriation at least a little bit

And still I'm not really getting IT, the fascination behind the inclusion to this is exclusive club

Truth be told it's one I'd rather not be a member of

Understand the membership fee comes in the form of my ancestor's history, that's a package deal.

Disgusting you could literally buy one before we got one freed!...Think!

And yet people seem to see this as a privilege instead of a curse

Do you really think we want the history that conceived this ugly word?

It's a bastard child fathered by a white slave master who then runs out and leaves us to raise the little nigger,

and yet people still can't seem to understand how this contributes to generations of black youths being run out on by father figures

Removing the father from the family was a common tactic back in the days of slavery

You give black their freedom and wonder why this practice keeps prevailing see,
It takes the piss, but it's just the word and if black people can say it then why can't white people say it,
and slavery that happened ages ago that was back when people used to be racist, goodness gracious no!
It is not just the word
it is an idea
you cannot kill an idea
ideas spread like Wildfire
it is a way of behaving
It is way of viewing yourself and others around you
it is less than
it is three fifths of a man
it is a salary cap
it is a life expectancy
it is only good for spitting bars on tracks
it is a fast track to Behind Bars
it is I can't
it is not a skin colour
it is a disease of the mind
And it will hold you down far more than chains ever could
And whether you spell IT "n-i-g-g-a or e-r, A & ER can only ever lead to sickness
Witness my fitness, my Roots Manuva all the way deep back into Africa's heart!
I'm just trying to embrace it into my veins the same way my foster parents let me into theirs

Love All That You Are

By Kelly Boyle

Beauty does not discriminate,
It has no singular definition,
Curvy, round, vivacious,
Small, tall, thin, slim,
Beauty does not care,
It sees you all there,
Shining out through eyes,
Smiles, hearts, actions,
It captures essence,
In our strengths, weaknesses, entwined,

To watch someone who is so full of doubt accept their own greatness,
A treasure of an experience,
To watch them acknowledge their own spirit,
To accept their core,
Take off the mask,
Watch them bloom,
Dip their toes in a world of liberation,
Hearts melt, eyes sparkle,
When you say, "I see you", "I accept you",
The mask is removed,

A mask created by external influence,
Un-acceptance of being and difference,
Words like knives,

Deeply imbedded,
Piercing self-esteem,
It filters through,
Creating internal beliefs,
Expectations that we should all be the same,
In those cages of words,

A complex web,
Enslaved, enraged, feeling powerless,
Portraying an unrealistic sense of weakness,
Disguising the reality of existence,
Body shaming,
As if to look a certain way makes you greater,
Made to feel inadequate,
Not fitting a preconceived mould,

But beauty does not discriminate,
Power, comfort, acceptability,
They're subjective to our own individual reality,
Because perfection is an illusion,
Chasing a dream that distracts us from living,
Our light shines bright,
My soul shall not shrink,
I accept my being,
The hairs on my chin,
The scars on my arms,
Representing all that I am,
My body, my vessel,
Takes care of me,
Getting me from A to B,

In return I've learnt to adore,

My curves, cellulite,

My emotional roar and badger-like hair,

Because Beauty does not discriminate,

It invigorates,

To recognise, to share,

To help nurture each other,

So we can grow, expand, blossom and bloom,

In a world that can be so unaccepting of difference,

Love ALL that you are!

My Philosophy

By Rana Jai Rajput aka Deelite MC

My Philosophy
I'm making way for atrocities,
Like the time
Satan changes face,
Call it technology
I'm coming through
My philosophy's based around visuals
Democracy is rotten
Africa raped for Gold and Cotton
Government be plotting
Like stopping research
Education leads to mass demonstrations
Exploitation by the ruling class....
GMO legislations
A bureaucrat's purpose

Time for role reversal
Make the rich poor, the poor rich
Two dimensions in a Third world
life's a bi***
Mass mind sickening, I'm picturing
Images of violence and pillages
A greedy world we're living in.
People starving and dying in villages
A sinister cause on Earth
Is Gods curse still harmless?
Should've saw Nostradamus' predictions

Pains inflicted, as we witness
Brutal monsters, with evil addictions

At the same time...
The U.N still be silent over rockets killing children
Political mind games and motives
Kids carry bags with explosives
Condoning
Israel arms that fight back
Call it War Crimes
A call of duty

Stopping racial genocide
Semitic Zionism
Call it Genesis
Peace in the Middle East
Looking for that Freedom, Justice, Equality
It's vital to get on board.
Military aided Isis crisis and war-zones leave you with
nightmares

How do we chase our dreams?
Why segregation, the classes?
Weapons for the masses?
It's beyond scope of comprehension.
Minds deep with a verse
In the universe we're just a speck
Empty words without the action
Mind rejects drowning in negative thoughts
Sceptics with limited awareness
Pace on,
Artistic and cultural movement renaissance
Corporate founders enslaved Africans,
They killed off Native Americans,
Bankrolled pirate ships,
Insured slave ships
And created Eugenics programs,

My Philosophy.

Kwansabas for Climate Justice

By Sai Murray

Flying above our planet you may pause.
How fragile. Where are the borders? Walls?
Shudder. Someone has left the gas on.
Are those candles for the Ogoni nine?
An eternal smogged flame for Saro-Wiwa?
Bonfire fury night and day where maps are drawn.
Protest hung. And village quartered.

Black death spawns a White saviour virus
Locusts take air, buzz over brown mouths
A bread basket is branded basket case.
Feed the world with helplss needy Afrikns.
Do they know it's thirty-four shopping days until Xmas?
Give us your fcking money!
How much a pith helmet space suit?

Steam release across Ocean.
//Sgrgatd city burns.
Nothing to see here in post-racial society.
Black Out this bleak Friday.
Buy nothing
Mammon clutches mama's throat.
//Hands up.
//Off.
Thick smoke revrses the choke hold.
//Cough.
Tears stream.
//Levees break, in these storms
a chance to remembr who we are.
Are you feeling Hot, Hot, Hot?

Are you feeling hot, hot, hot?

By Miles Chambers

(An extract)

Big shout! Jump up! Do the bogle, the limbo and a Calypso spin!
Braid your hair, fashion a style, find some flashy costume to put your dancing legs in.
It's me, Milo, with a tale wicked and wild, are you feeling hot, hot, hot?
Mek I tell you the SP on St Paul's Carnival, the full story, how much time have you got?
Carnival started as a church, community fete, let me see, can I remember the specific date?
It was to celebrate the St Paul's community, Father Bernard and his elders organised it, sometime in 1968.
The 80's brought change, the breddas in St Paul's stood up to oppression they got serious and tuff
There were racial riots in St Paul's, times were hard, the brothers said enough is enough
St Paul's was the frontline, place of refuge, the Rastas stated; "Is my yard dis, ah fe we place!"
After the uprising, Rastas from Inkworks gave carnival an Afro Caribbean face.

Caribbean carnivals came from mass, the enslaved dressed up and mocked the masters, for one day a year.

They paraded their costumes and flamboyant attire, had fun, on that day they showed no fear.

Stop the proceedings, lick wood, shoot up two or three in the air. Stand big and bold.

The 90's was a high time! Radio One wanted to buy in, carnival was ready to explode.

1,000,000 of funding, Tim Westwood, Trevor Nelson, and Chris Goldfinger wanted to be a part of the act.

Nelson Mandela was freed, and Mandela's Hideway was made in St Agnes Park to mark this historic act.

Macka B and Frankie Paul played, carnival could have become really really big

Let's get together and feel alright, The Bob Marley theme, that was a special gig.

Carlton, Kwesi and Afredos took leave, energy left for a while, but carnival soon found its pride

Carnival was the first to bring black stand comedy to Bristol and make us chuckle deep inside...

Carnival is moving on, based at Ceed, it just recently celebrated its anniversary,

Pax has brought a new flair. The processions are bigger and better, they're planning a carnival academy.

Unity in our diversity, is our strength. Let's celebrate Afro Caribbean culture with the whole community,

LET all in Bristol hold bogle & Calypso dance competitions and have bulla cake with their afternoon tea.

So... people, whether you're a long man, short man, rich man, poor man, or just got out on probation.

Whether you're an artisan, a nurse administering medication, a radio DJ or an honest politician.

Whether your name is Pax, Steve, Alfredos, Kwesi Carlton, Edson, Bertel, Sally, Chris, Sara, Garfield,

Tim, Friztroy, James, Collette Kwentengee, Elaine, Christine, Doris. Nuff man me na mention.

Whether your sound system's called Toyboy, Unique Star, Iquator, Qualitex, Imperial Force, Wild Bunch, Fergy, Lakota.

If you're drinking; Ribena, Dragon Stout, Red Stripe, Nourishment, Supermalt, smoothie, lemonade or coffee...

Boogie... yea man boogie... to the St Paul's Carnival possie!

Inner Peace

By Shareefa Energy

What Does Peace Look Like?
Peace within yourself
Peace and contentment
Heart at ease
No sudden disruptions.
What does peace taste like?
Like fresh lemonade under a clear blue sky.
What does it mean to be grounded?
To be living aligned and in your purpose.
What does my inner world look like?
Is it chaotic
Volcanic
Ready to rupture and explode at the slight nudge of an
uninvited breeze?
What does peace look like?
Uneasily swayed by surrounding noise
Resistant and resilient from absorbing energies and
emotions.
Conjuring a shield between the wounded when staying
focused on your own healing.
What does peace look like?
Chakras aligned, a mesmerising fountain within
Shades of magenta and burnt orange
Comforting and soothing.
What does peace look like?
What does your inner world look like?

Will a retrograde catapult create a frenzy?
Will it bring to surface what needs to be buried and
breathing its final breath?
What does peace look like?

Stone Home

By Saju Ahmed

Sometimes I can look like stone to outsiders
Do you know the feeling of hearts grinding into asphalt?
Skin black as tar pressed with heat, moulding me to fit in
thin, fire in my eyes explodes like petrol bombs
my lovers sway with my curves, after all they know me best
feel my ribs cracking under pressure,
As a stampede of migrant feet flee to me
my rebellion is the reason why they are still breathing

Chapeltown, Harehills…
They see me as home but outside see something foreign.
A rebellion against the English look
As the night fuelled with fire, racism, poverty
But our rebellion wasn't violence
The phoenix dances in my guts
To the rhyme of David Hamilton's dream
Feel the vibrations with RJC

My rebellion wasn't bricks and stones
Leeds Young Authors speak on my tongue,
Sparked by the thoughts of Khadijah Ibrahiim and Paulette
Morris, allowing young poets pen to ink over borders and
margins.
My rebellion is the Sunday practise,
A stage that doesn't censor me, makes sense to me.

You young folk mind the gap on your journey,
It's not radio hype when I'm saying they stereotype you -
My rebellion is up and down my spine, it's the carnival song in my chest
My rebellion is Roundhay Park at the reach of my arms.
Listening to Michael Jackson sing,
My feet move smooth to migration, but feel the burn of lost souls.

My rebellion isn't guns and blood,
It is locking my palms in pray,
Fingers allowing a Mosque to join a Church,
While eating together in a Gurdwara.
As the Rasta greets you in the name of him

My rebellion isn't English, it's my mixed tongue, Patois, Bangla, Hindi, Punjabi , Polish, Yoruba, Shona, NDEBELE, Urdu, Cantonese.
My rebellion isn't separation, but unity through the part of me we laid to rest.
The sign home for the children that found harbour on my part of Leeds, on my part of the roads.

Her Name is Hip-Hop

By Tanya Muneera Williams

Me:
As it was in the beginning - so shall it be in the
end, everyone deserves to right to express,I rather be
breathless - seconds away from death than left without the
means to mediate my emotions and sing a song for those
folk who had been broken,
minutes before dawn or blood choking,
or the man dem and the yout dem out on the corner toking,
because no-one ever told they could achieve, in this world
where we've all been deceived and the only bit of reality
comes from the undersigned emcee..

Him:
Piece of a man, ghetto prophet, speaking of philosophical
sonic in the language somewhere between cockney and
ebonics,
over boombox beatbox or beats electronic.
Lovable rogue modern day sage with the swagger not just
saved for the stage he reps everyone -   from the cradle to
the grave.
Yet nay sayers say in these days man's got a get paid.
He's become a slave - to the psychology of C-R-E-A-M that
taught our sons that alone should you dream.
 another mother cries,
 another son has died,

And our daughters are preoccupied with Hip-Hop honeys
and playboy bunnies and it's kind of funny how the tale of
the tragic mulatto still exist
If only she could click, click, click her heels and emerge on
the other side of the rainbow,
with her soul intact, before the yellow brick road
there will be no trusted companions like Toto,
but there will be dogs 'tho,
you know those 'breahs' with the high libidos,
and their jaws open wide so,
who want to hit that bumper like it was the Bongo

"what you saying, what you saying,
come we do a combo
 just don't be expecting no phone calls tomorrow
 I roll with the crew killers like we in the Congo
 we carry knives and borers and run loco
Killing can ourselves softly in sloooooo-moooooo"

Just some get out of the ghetto type of blues, some get out
to ghetto type of blues, the type of blues they don't put in
the news or the type of blues that gets distorted in the
news.
But this ain't the movies and I don't know how I got the
blame,
the hip-hop that you know it's not the hip-hop that's in my
name,
the hip-hop that's in my veins,
my hip pop how do I describe -

Her:

My hip pop used to have extensions in her hair bamboo
earrings at least two pairs,

she's a inspiration for coco butter tho at the times she can
provoke a brother as she's passing him by

come with me,

she's got to be the best thing since stocks in Clarks
Wallabies

she's taught many an emcees to be ultra and magnetic,
every rappers delight,

 I used to love her and I still do because she's so -

Adidas she's so Carharrt jacket and baggy jeans,

she's so door-knocker earrings me in my early teens

she's so everything you could conjure up in your dreams,

so is it her or us running to extremes,

a reflection of society and she always has been

just like her older brother reggae I

she's not a has been and she's never has been she's not a
has been and she's never has been,

It's just that when it comes to our culture my friends, you
and I, we have been had.

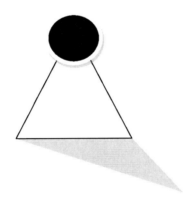

In Search of a King and Identity

By Roger Griffith

Yet society could not find a place for me,
A scientist or a scholar I felt I could not be.

Why there was a blank page in my school book remained a
mystery,
As I began my self-taught search for history.

For as a poor uneducated angry youth,
Prison, the army an unmarked grave I felt was my destiny,
yes I really was that uncouth.

And so in my quest for salvation I turned away from these
hostile lands,
To a place where Lady Liberty stands.

There I had connections through my blood lines which gave
me an aura,
A shared sense heritage from the African diaspora.

Floetry

By Dominic Heslop (AKA Thee Devoted One)

For a living I do spoken word.
So a voice is heard.
Not just mine, I mean yours too
If your vocals work.
It's an art form that proportions purpose,
Which coordinates verses.
So don't ask me on the axis of why I do this,
As X marks the spot to my future,
Where souls can attain worthy.
Young and old can remain sturdy
In all they believe because without goals it's a draw.
But I'm sure the whole point of the game is to score.
I'm that certain.
'Cause we all want our names on the board.
Proclaimed to be great by maiden or sir.
And I'm not saying, that whether or not that day will occur,
your less of a brain to the world. I mean,
It's motivation that's making you work,
Creating a surge that's awaiting emergence.
But would you still do what you do if nobody rated your curve?
With all the time that it's taken you to learn?
And could you still move forward without being failure deterred?
As I perceive, that's what's making you a person.

Implanted in your own two feet reliant on what they say to makes you worth it. George Elliot said –
"It's never too late to be what you might have been."
So I say why delay to be of service?
Procrastination needs to be unheard of.
But I can't speak on the means that I'm wording,
'Cause it's taken years for me to word this.
Esteem got the best of my dreams,
Suppressed in my sleep, unsettled by the demons,
Wrestled and I'm weak, pressured by the streets,
'Cause deprivation makes a feral belly eat.
But it's incredible to me
How I went from that para guy with no composure,
Only a hammer and knife to mold my sculpture,
that even tower guys have never thought of,
As only the talent lies in my closed book,
which I'm now opening to show ya.
Title - Thee Devoted One.

Celf

By Johnny Albrow aka J Zill

Listen, you need to find yourcelf,
Be genuine with mind, benign to celf,
Or your gonna end up miles behind yourcelf,
Recline, that's fine, but first apply yourcelf,
Aligned to cloud nine, that's your higher celf.
I heard you're scared of freezing up, passion's fire helps, but
don't scorch your wealth, that's a crime to celf. Sometimes I
need to keep a sharp eye on celf, because I is celf-less, and
tired of welts, from those who misuse and lie to celf, supply
the type of vibe that're cyanide to celf,
I try stay far away, high on shelf, but I keep coming down to
say 'Hi', oh well. Celf with a C, because that's how science
spells, at least it should do,
'Cause all we are is piles of cells, so cells create celf, that's
how I've felt, since that KRS lecture,
I've seen a crowd excel, at chasing short skirts,
Forget a quiet celf, I celf is funny to me
like that guy Chappelle, Pisces sign but feel
a Gemini in celf, evil twin on the verge
of taking over this shell. What you need to do is truly admire
celf, that way you can only multiply
your-celf, expand like weed strands and G5 fly
through celf. But before all that
look in the mirror, now smile at celf :)

My Kings and Heroes

By Roger Griffith

For his re-education Malcolm Little became Malcolm X of
the nation,
Until he was killed by some brothers, in Harlem in an
altercation.

X too marked the spot that made King's foot-soldiers cross,
When they entered the ballot box.

I learned of leaders like Mandela sent to jail for challenging
Apartheid, at times a fugitive he had to hide in caves.
And of Fredrick Douglass the first Black visitor to the White
House, which resident Michele Obama told me was built by
slaves.

I discovered what had brought these Kings & Queens to the
States and Caribbean nations,
Were in the words of Trinidad Premier Eric Williams,
commerce and early globalisations.

The land of the free it dawned on me was the home to the
braves and slaves,
As proud Arawak's, Nubian, Taino, Akan, Caribs, and Igbos,
all succumbed to men from across the waves.

Millions of Africans transported worse than cattle,
Through the sickening Middle Passage to face a new battle.

Across the Americas their lives like ashes were scattered,
With dreams of family life, civilisations and riches forever
shattered.

To the Caribbean chain of islands my peoples were sent,
To live a life less than well spent.

Those slaves rose to become freed,
But that was the bare minimum need.

For the Colonial rulers failed to invest,
Yet the Empire still reaped dividends from their fruitful
harvest.

CONTRIBUTOR BIOGRAPHIES

1.   **Anndeloris Marina Chacon** is a charity manager and support worker with carers and the community. "Something has relit the fire" within her soul. Through the response of the community another passion returned, and she has started to write again on life and its journeys. Listening has been the key that has opened doors for herself and those about her. She states: "We need to rebuild communication in the communities with trust and respect for everyone." Google or find Anndeloris Chacon on Linkedin.com

2.   **Alexia Lindsay aka Humble Be** is from West Brom but is now based in Bristol. She rolls with the punches, but started writing to express herself after visiting dark places and being uncertain about the challenges she faced. She writes for joy and optimism, but is taking on her adverse demons. Through this outlet she hopes to shed light on situations while being determined not to continue beating herself up. Eventually she has convinced herself she has much to offer in terms of resolution, which may contribute to a better environment for all.

3.   **Alyx Tamminen** hails from Hull. Her strong Northern voice has represented at Spoken Word nights across the country. She does festivals, and has attended Freedom and Humber Mouth. A working class feminist, she was introduced to the local poetry scene by a showing of Allen Ginsberg's 'Howl'. Her style is quirky, fast paced and

rhythmic with influences from the hip hop she listens to far too much of.

4.   **Charmaine Lawrence**, writes powerful Poetry from experience, and is a cultured entrepreneur grounded in her Bristol community. Her mantras are: "Learn everyday in the flow of life. Be grateful and humble, and aim to live up to my fullest potential." Find her at Mogul Minded Group.

5.   **Chloe Rose Laing**, now established in Bristol, describes herself as a 'Vessel of Song' with a voice that "echoes sultry notes of expressive and hypnotic rhythms." Her vibe is poetic, as she blends word and sound into a new genre called Roots Afro Soul. Inspired by the ancestral cries of our foremothers and fathers. Her spiritualised piece within this book appeals to all. She collaborates with others yet remains true to her Celtic and Afro-Caribbean background. See ww.chloeroselaing.com

6.   **Cleo Alberta Lake** – is a Bristolian Art-ivist of Afro and Scottish roots, winner of the ADAD award, explores themes of Carnival, Masquerade, collective Dance energy, history and rebellion. She's a writer, film maker, collage artist, actress and was involved in producing Foundations (Bristol) and Journey of the Griot at Colston Hall's opening event. She was a writer in residence at the Arnolfini. "I'm driven by truth and justice," she advises. www.arnolfini.org.uk/blog/sweet-sea-mask

7.   **David Punter** is a poet and critic. He has published five small collections: *China and Glass* (Bran's Head Press), *Asleep at the Wheel* (Amani), *Lost in the Supermarket* (Open Heart Press), *Selected Short Stories* and *Foreign Ministry* (both Hub Editions), and poems in many journals and magazines. He is currently Co-Director of the Bristol Poetry Institute.

8.   **Dan Audio** is a poet, singer-song writer and a recorded musician, as well as a frontman. He's released a strong repertoire of great work and performs passionately. He fuses combinations of Rap, Soul, Funk, Blues and Rock, keeping it real to who he is (with a working class swagger), and where he's from. His vibe has been promoted worldwide by Tuff Gong, yep, you heard that right. He's sold a whole heap of albums. His band Pusher have supported All Saints and Travis.

9.   **Dareece James** is a young Bristol based poet who has been writing from a young age. She began performing at 15 after winning a Simon Powell Poetry Prize. She has gone on to present her work at various events including conferences and networking events. Her major themes embrace ethnicity and gender, family and social issues. She is currently finishing a Masters.

10.   **Dominic Heslop, aka Thee Devoted One,** is a young spoken word artist of Jamaican heritage from Sheffield, South Yorkshire. His passion is reaching the younger generation through mentoring and encouraging self-

expression to help them stay on, or come back to the right path. Dominic has set up the Slam Barz hip hop and spoken word event in Sheffield to support youths with these aims. https://soundcloud.com/limiteddevotion/tracks

11. **Henna CanPoetry**, Manchester based, is a Freelance spoken word poet who embarked within the world of poetry during a nomadic point in her life. As a radio and TV presenter, she believes in the Open Road, and her poetry is based upon a spiritual perspective of a Nomad. She can appear everywhere and anywhere – providing the politics are agreeable. Google Henna CanPoetry.

12. **Joel Douglas aka Splitz P** is a Jamaican Pakistani, hailing from Bristol. Smooth, current and engaging, he uses music, spoken word, and youth orientated projects to engage with the community. He does radio appearances (UJIMA and BBC), and live performance of his work. soundcloud.com/splitzpuk Instagram.com/splitzp

13. **Hannah Teasedale** was born and bred in Birmingham. Her writing has been described as 'heart-breaking', 'raw', 'knotty', and 'honest and brutal'. She does not shy away from exposing her truth, as uncomfortable as it is. A Mistress in creative writing, she has two previous poetry collections published: 'Fingerprints' by Poetry Space in 2013 and 'Laid Bare' by Burning Eye in 2016, and is currently working on a cross-genre short novel, 'Sharp Things'. Google Hannah M Teasedale.

14. **Jasmine Ketibuah Foley, aka Jazz,** is a Musician, broadcast journalist and presenter on BCFM and Ujima radio. She is also currently a social researcher as a Green and Black Ambassador looking into ethnic diversity in the 'Green sector.' Furthermore, she challenges "large organisations and communities on inclusivity in matters of environmentalism and sustainability."
www.mixcloud.com/thespaceproject

15. **Johnny Albrow, aka J Zill,** is a 17 year old MC, poet, producer and beat maker from the Steel City. He has performed with the likes of Otis Mensah and Jay Clique, and on BBC Sheffield Introducing. His style adds to the cement mix of Hip Hop music spewed out and slapped on every brick and stone in the city's beating heart. www.grey-don.bandcamp.com

16. **Kabbo Ferdinand Van Tura** lives in Bristol, and is an Artivist, story teller, youth worker, journalist, writer, theatre practitioner, healer, film maker and writer. He uses a variety of Indigenous First Nation Knowledge Systems; fusing these techniques with Performing Arts Methods in combination with Eastern Disciplines & cinema. His helpful intentions are to build safe, playful platforms that allow us to initiate cultural interventions - encouraging self-acceptance and healing. On Facebook: Ferdinand Kabbo Van Tura.

17. **Kelly Boyle**, now in Leeds, is a songwriter/performer and Visual Artist from Wakefield. Her work "reflects a personal journey of self-awareness and

progression of finding balance between my emotive and logical nature. Influenced by surrounding frequencies, environments and everything else that I absorb on the way;" www.kellyboyle.co.uk

18.   **Lawrence Hoo, aka Hoo Law,** is a Bristol based poet. He states: "My work is influenced by various experiences of growing up in and around Easton and St Paul's, where I'm exposed to a medley of culture, identity and heritage. The impact of social imbalance on minority communities has had a deep and lasting impression on what I do." He has developed short films, worked with young people, curated exhibitions and published two collections of poetry: 'Inner City Tales' and 'Hoostory'. He was Ujima Radio's poet in residence and has been working on several projects using poetry, film and a novel. "I'm currently developing an art installation with 8th Sense Media." https://www.facebook.com/LawrenceHooUk

19.   **Lauren Living Harrison**, from London, says: "I'm the entity that wakes you from your dreams as you're falling, just about to hit the ground." She's well connected and determined to make an impact through creative expression, with links to the great youth debate movement and independent artists and promoters. On Facebook: Lauren Living Harrison.

20.   **Miles Chambers** from Wiltshire is now Bristol's 1st City Poet laureate, as named by his friend and current Mayor Marvin Rees (2016/17). He was a Presenter at Ujima

Radio 98fm, with his own Lyrical Genius show. He has studied Visual Culture at University and knows how to cook a great meal, as well as concoct a riveting poem about where he's from and where he's at, and he never quite loses sight of both. He has claimed that Bristol is "full of paradoxes." Catch up with Miles online via Google.

21.   **MfyahSis MC** is a young creator. "I love words; I have a special connection with them. I also love knowledge and knowledge comes into this earth in many ways. For me, words are one of the pathways into the Earth's secrets. Through discussions, debate, and likewise I realise I have a message to share, and rap is one of the ways I can share it... I believe people have to feel what you are expressing to get it through, so I believe in words that are hot with meaning and expression."

22.   **Mama D** equals mother, and the word 'mother', as she states, "according to the traditional knowledge of the Yoruba people, depicts the place located between *Orun* (Heaven) and *Aye* (Earth), a place of transformations and transcendence." That is the wordology of Mama D, translated from Africa to the Americas and then back across the Atlantic to the UK. Central to all the work she does, either on the land, within communities, with spirit or with herself, is the understanding that healing is essential to both outcome and process, for all of our livity, here upon Mother Earth. See mamadimensions.wordpress.com

23.   **Meshach R Brencher**, a former Young Identity writer's group member, is from Manchester where he's honed his imperious talent. He's a teacher, curator, a performance artist and writer, exploring identity, human condition, depression, domestic situations, and the environment. He writes poetry, monologues and flash fiction. His work has featured in Common-word's 'Elevator Fiction' Micro Narrative Anthology in 2016, and 'Sweet Tongues' in 2013, and he was a part of 'Battle of the Minds' at the Contact Theatre at the Manchester Literature Festival. He also performed spoken word for the 'Chaos to Order' music project in May 2015, and co-wrote and performed in 'Stagnant Change' in 2015.
http://meshachbrencher.wixsite.com/mysite

24.   **Nathaniel** 'Superbeastmode' **Benson-Goodyear** was born in Leeds 1999. "I've had the honour to represent Leeds young authors at the brace new voices international poetry slam and be a member of the Ralph Thoresby slam team, taking home victory at the 2012 shake the dust national youth poetry slam." Proud to be a poet.

25.   **Nattylyn Jeffers** resides in Leeds, from Bedfordshire, a 3rd Generation Jamaican and Vincentian, She is an acclaimed contemporary cultural performance artist & a Restorative Complementary Holistic Therapist , a Nubian Mother who strives to promote positive practices for those facing societal oppression. She obtains a Master of Arts in Youth and Community Development, "From de

Rastafarian (Tribe of Joseph), a true Humanitarian..."
Twitter: @nattylyn Facebook - italrootsandhealing

26.   **Rana Jai Rajput,** aka Deelite MC, based in Leicester started as a garage MC. He works musically, live, and was BBC Asian Network feature Artist on several occasions. He performs at big city Melas and has worked with Real Tone Records and Baby Blu. Now focused on Desi infused urban beats he maintains conscious themes.
https://www.facebook.com/deelitemc

27.   **Razor** is in Bristol, a young up-and-coming UK based Hip Hop artist and producer. He creates socio-political messages in songs, reflecting, "what goes on in today's society", and raps about everyday life experience. He volunteers with many different youth organisations including Freedom Project, and has supported Linton Kwesi Johnson at Colston Hall, and through all his efforts hopes he can make a difference to his Bristol community.

28.   **Rebecca Tantony**, although Bristol based, crosses borders, as her poetry can be about anything and anywhere depending on where she goes. Her work tells deep and meaningful stories that represent and reach different communities. She's performed at various venues from the Royal Albert Hall to The Arnolfini, and was inspired by early Hip Hop. Associated with Apples and Snakes, Harbourside Festival and others, as a poetry event hostess, she's dedicated. Her poetic flash non-fiction collection, 'Talk You Round Till Dusk' was published by Burning Eye Books,

as was her latest collection, 'All The Journeys I Never Took.' She is an associate lecturer in Performance Poetry at Bath Spa University. The Guardian has described her work as, "Mesmerising."

29.   **Rob Mitchell** – Poet, Producer and Educator, has lived in various places. "I am a Creative Media Producer who studied Drama in Bristol and then used media mainly as a tool for engaging people and communities, often with the aims of learning and civic participation. Co-founder of Firstborn Creatives with Shawn Sobers and former of director Black Pyramid Film and Video Project. His work considers history and belonging.
robbymitch.wordpress.com

30.   **Roger Griffith** - a social entrepreneur, delivers community and social action projects. He co-runs award winning Ujima Radio CIC where he is also a broadcaster. He also leads a community consultancy 2morrow 2day connecting business. He's concerned with consultation, media, employment and diversity projects. In the 1980's Roger experienced unemployment before rediscovering education, then moved from trainee to senior manager in local government where he specialised in social housing and empowering communities. He published his first book 'My American Odyssey-From the Windrush to the White House in 2015. Further he is an artistic producer, writes for cultural magazine Bristol 24/7, and is a film curator - rogergriffith.co.uk, rogergriffithwriter@gmail.com and Twitter @rogerg44.

31.   **Russ Litten** is hails from current City of Culture, Hull. He writes novels, short stories and poems. He writes for TV, film, radio and the stage. He's a regular tutor at Arvon Writing Courses and a workshop tutor for First Story in a secondary school. In 2016 Russ, along with the internationally renowned producer and musician Steve Cobby, released the spoken word/electronica album "My People Come from the Sea". A collection named "We Know What We Are" (Wrecking Ball Press) is due. Facebook Russ Litten or visit www.russlitten.com or www.smashwords.com/profile/view/russlitten

32.   **Ricky Venel Stone** was born and raised in Birmingham to Jamaican parents. Studied Graphic Design, moved to Leeds after graduating and started performing hip hop, soul and jazz inspired poetry. He has also worked as a Poet Coach. In recent years, since becoming a father, he writes when inspired and plays percussion.

33.   **Saju Iqbal Ahmed** featured in Volume 1, a Slam champion Spoken word poet and rapper from Leeds associated with Leeds Young Authors, Lyrically Justified volume 2's chosen charity. He done BBC 1xtra and featured in acclaimed documentaries including We are Poets. He's performed up and down the UK and well as internationally and shines with great delivery and content reflecting local and international life and it's barriers human success, integration and co-operation.. FB Saju Ahmed Iqbal for more.

34.　　**Sai Murray** is a Leeds based writer, spoken word artist, and graphic designer of Bajan/Afrikan/English heritage. His first poetry collection Ad-liberation, was published in 2013. He was lead writer on Virtual Migrants 2015 touring production, Continent Chop Chop and runs artist/activist promotions agency Liquorice Fish. He is a poet facilitator on Voices that Shake; a Numbi resident poet; and arts and politics editor of Sable Lit Mag @saimurai saimurai.wordpress.com

35.　　**Shareefa Energy** (aka Shareefa Grassroots) is a London based Hip-Hop inspired spoken word performance poet, writer, workshop facilitator, aspiring actress and playwright of Indian heritage from Highfields, Leicester. She explores women's and migrant community issues, moving audiences, provoking spiritual and mental growth. To add to her awards she recently won best UEA Poet 2017. She released her spoken word EP 'Reasoning with Self' in 2015. Her poetry featured on Channel 4 for National Poetry Day. She's also the founder of the spoken word play 'Wombs Cry.' www.shareefaenergy.com

36.　　**Steve Deegan** is a songwriter, poet, multi-instrumentalist and music producer from Liverpool. He studied modern languages in Leeds, where he lived over a decade, playing in numerous bands, fronting the Royal Park Orchestra and Roguish Stranger, and refining his art. His awards include Bright Young Things and UK Songwriting Contest. He has lived in France, Spain, Portugal and Senegal, and continues to produce original lyrical music as a solo artist, Moving Sands.

37.   **Lucy Clark** is your typical Hull lass come BBC local radio presenter, tackling the everyday qualms in life such as doing your 'Big Shop' at the supermarket, the sights at your local gym, or even the way food is served nowadays. Lucy says what we're all thinking, in rhyme, whilst showing great proudness for her home City of Hull, which you'll get from most of her poems.

38.   **Solomon OB**, 2016's Hammer and Tongue Slam champion, has performed extensively, was crowned by BBC 1extra and Roundhouse London Words Finalist, and continues to be noted as an acclaimed young spoken word poet and frontman, constantly on the move, leaving him difficult to pin down. He's has a rounded delivery, and connects with his audiences left, right, and centre. He recently featured on Ted talks with 'Spoken Word as a crossroad to happiness,' as well as wrote and performed "Bridging the Tracks" for BBC Sports TV, dedicated to the 2017 London Olympics. Find his Hip Hop Funk band Sounds of Harlowe online. www.twitter.com/solomon

39.   **Sukina Douglas** is a UK London based Spoken Word Poet, Dreamer, Wife, Emcee, Pilgrim, Educator, Nomad, Seeker, Sufi, Event Organizer, and Cafe Supervisor at **Poetry Cafe**. Born in Bristol and the other half of Poetic Pilgrimage Hip Hop duo who have performed across the UK, Europe, the USA, North and South Africa sharing their unique

conscious poetry to engage communities. From a rich and colourful background, she has been and keeps herself very busy.

40. **Tanya Muneera Williams**, of mixed heritage was born and raised in Bristol although currently based in London. She's half of a duo called Poetic Pilgrimage and reflects her UK roots, as well as her journey as a Muslim and relationship to hip hop. Since 2011 she's appeared at various locations around the world including Africa, America and Europe, spreading their vibes. The group have done TV appearances, and supported Talib Kweli and K'naan. "These girls work hard to challenge stereotypes, redefine what's cool and bring back the feel good vibe to Hip Hop whilst maintaining the message in the music." Seek PoeticPilgrimageMusic online

41. **Tom Burgess** focuses on the environment, play and transformation. Among other things he is a mentor for OPAL (Outdoor Play and Learning) and head of activities at Marlborough College School of English and Culture. Tom writes and performs poetry, his work linking to the landscape, urban or natural. His poetry collection 'Paint Yourself' was recently published by Arkbound. tompburgess.blogspot.co.uk/

42. **Waltraud Pospischil aka Firebird** is based in Bristol. She's a poet, artist and writer. "I've been an Equality Rep in Bristol. Writing poetry is for me a matter of survival - like talking to an imaginary friend." Born to WW2 refugee

parents in Austria, from a young age she's been scared of wars and all the destruction that entails, "I once wrote letters for Amnesty International at the age of 14" and believes "if we don't have a world for everybody where all people are equal, - I don't belong here..."
outsidein.org.uk/Waltraud-Pospischil